Christmas in Heaven

Copyright 2011 © by Donna Beserra
All rights reserved
ISBN: 978-0-9982826-0-2

This book is a work of fiction. Any resemblances to actual persons, living or dead, or actual events is purely coincidental.

Scripture quotation was taken from the King James Version Bible.

DEDICATION

This book is dedicated to those whose loved ones have left this world to be in Heaven with Jesus. The bible tells us in John 3:16: "For God so loved the world, that he gave his only begotten Son, that whosoever believeth in him should not perish, but have everlasting life."

This book has also been written in hopes that those who don't know Jesus, will come to know him as their Lord and Savior.

Christmas in Heaven

Written and Illustrated by:
Donna Beserra

It was two weeks before Christmas and six-year-old Julie was full of anticipation. Her parents, Dave and Carol had taught little Julie about the true meaning of Christmas. Carol would always read the bible story of Christ's birth. Then the family would pray and sing Happy Birthday to Jesus before opening their gifts.

Sadly, this year Carol had become very ill. The doctor was doing everything he could, but he was wasn't giving poor Carol very much hope. If she was lucky, she might make it through the holiday season. Dave and Carol were praying for a miracle. The couple tried their best to remain positive. They didn't want to frighten their daughter, but the little girl knew her mother was sick. Being a child, Julie just expected her mom to get well.

Julie wanted to get her mother an extra special gift, something that would make Carol feel better. While shopping with her dad, Julie came across the perfect Christmas gift for Carol. Julie spotted a picture of Jesus. It was set in a frame that had a light shining brightly on his face. Julie jumped joyously.

"Daddy, this picture will make Mom feel better! She loves Jesus. This way she can look at his picture every day." Dave paid for the gift, and they took it home and wrapped it.

Unfortunately, Carol's condition worsened. A week before Christmas, Carol died. Dave was devastated. Now he would have to break the news to his beloved daughter.

Dave took little Julie in his arms and explained that her mother had gone to Heaven to be with Jesus. Julie understood that she would not see her mother again in this world. Grandma, Grandpa and Uncle Ben had already gone to Heaven, and Julie hadn't seen them since. Julie cried hysterically.

In spite of his grief, Dave tried to pull himself together for Julie's sake. Julie was heartbroken. She didn't laugh. She didn't play. She just moped around and cried at the drop of a hat.

Christmas Day arrived. The home was lonely and quiet. Julie looked miserable. Dave felt helpless. He tried his best to comfort his daughter. Then, just when the situation seemed hopeless, an unexpected smile came across Julie's face.

"Jesus must be really happy today Daddy!" Julie grinned.

"What do you mean honey?" Dave inquired.

"Mama's spending Christmas with him. They must be having a really big birthday party; and Grandma, Grandpa and Uncle Ben are all there. They must be singing Happy Birthday to Jesus right now."

Dave's child had just shown him a whole new perspective. He hugged his daughter.

Julie unwrapped the gift she had gotten her mother. That night, Julie set the picture on her nightstand. It would always be a reminder that Julie's Mom was with Jesus, and would be celebrating Christmas in Heaven.

For more information about Heaven, read the bible.

Grandpa

Grandma

Uncle Ben

www.ingramcontent.com/pod-product-compliance
Lightning Source LLC
Chambersburg PA
CBHW041126300426
44113CB00002B/79